# SPEAK UP!
### CONFRONTING DISCRIMINATION IN YOUR DAILY LIFE™

# CONFRONTING
# ABLEISM

## SUSAN NICHOLS

**Rosen**
**YA**
™

New York

Published in 2018 by The Rosen Publishing Group, Inc.
29 East 21st Street, New York, NY 10010

First Edition

**Library of Congress Cataloging-in-Publication Data**

Names: Nichols, Susan, 1975 – author.
Title: Confronting ableism / Susan Nichols.
Description: New York: Rosen Publishing, 2018. | Series:
Speak up! Confronting discrimination in your daily life |
Includes bibliographical references and index. | Audience:
Grades 7–12.
Identifiers: LCCN 2017015792| ISBN 9781538381625
(library bound) | ISBN 9781538381601 (pbk.) | ISBN
9781538381618 (6 pack)
Subjects: LCSH: Discrimination against people with
disabilities—United States—Juvenile literature. | People with
disabilities—United States–Juvenile literature.
Classification: LCC HV1553 .N53 2018 | DDC
305.9/080973–dc23
LC record available at https://lccn.loc.gov/2017015792

*Manufactured in China*

# CONTENTS

# INTRODUCTION

**H**istorians like to point out that the United States was founded on principles of freedom. Every American has the right to life, liberty, and the pursuit of happiness, according to Thomas Jefferson's words in the Declaration of Independence. However, that has not always been true. In fact, it was not true at the time the declaration was signed because many Americans were suffering under slavery and women had few legal rights compared with men. Slavery was legally abolished in 1863, when Abraham Lincoln signed the Emancipation Proclamation, and women were granted the right to vote in 1920. Of course, those were positive legal developments, but they did not instantly correct the everyday discrimination that people experienced.

Over the last sixty years in the United States, Americans have become more aware of the ways in which their fellow citizens may still not enjoy the rights to which they are entitled. For example, during the civil rights movement of the 1950s and 1960s, Americans moved to ensure that African Americans' rights to vote, attend school, and work were protected. In the 1970s, an active women's rights movement made progress in highlighting the discrimination that existed against women. Gay and lesbian Americans saw their right to marry earn federal recognition in 2015 when the Supreme Court ruled gay marriage legal.

This protest led by ADAPT, an organization that defends the rights of disabled Americans, was held in front of the White House in 2009. It called for President Obama to pass the Community Choice Act with health care reforms.

There is one group in particular whose rights are still not fully recognized, however—and its members are numerous. One in every five Americans has a disability, according to a 2012 US Census Bureau report. That means that 56.7 million people, or almost 20 percent of the population, are disabled in some way. Some people have multiple disabilities, and many have disabilities that are severe and that prohibit their ability to fully participate in a normal lifestyle.

Some Americans have disabilities that require assistance in their everyday activities. For example, a blind person may need another person or a specially trained dog to help him or her be mobile and travel. Still other Americans have disabilities that may seem "invisible" to those who are unaware of them. For example, according to the US Census Bureau, "About 19.9 million people [have] difficulty lifting and grasping. This includes, for instance, trouble lifting an object like a bag of groceries, or grasping a glass or a pencil." It

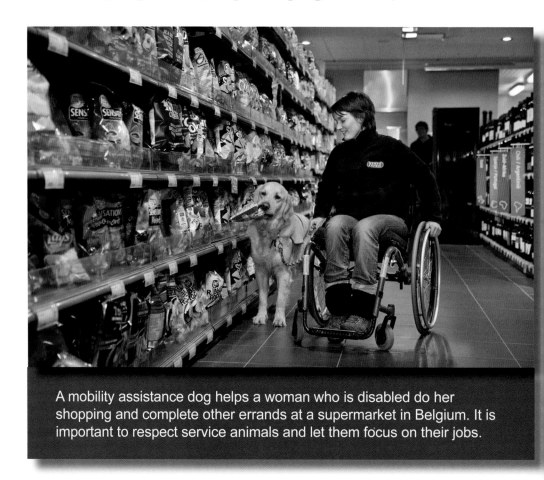

A mobility assistance dog helps a woman who is disabled do her shopping and complete other errands at a supermarket in Belgium. It is important to respect service animals and let them focus on their jobs.

is more difficult to see this type of disability in another person, but it obviously is a problem that can prevent that person from completing everyday, routine activities.

Despite this tremendous number, Americans with disabilities are frequently discriminated against in their lives. While many Americans are becoming more aware or sensitive to discrimination experienced by people in terms of race, gender, ethnicity, and religion, some are still unaware of the ways in which disabled Americans are ostracized and their rights denied.

# CHAPTER ONE

# DEFINING ABLEISM

Discrimination is defined as "the unjust treatment of different categories of people or things, especially on the basis of factors like race, age, religious affiliation, or sex." In a nation that prides itself on protecting every citizen's right to life, liberty, and the pursuit of happiness, it is important to understand that, while nobody can tell a person how to feel about a group of people, discrimination is against the law.

For example, a person may have a bias and feel prejudiced against a certain group of people, such as women, Jews, or Asian Americans. However, that person may not legally treat someone from that group differently because of his or her feelings. In another example, a company owner may unjustly feel that a certain group of people is lazy, but he or she may not deny a person from that group an equal chance for a job at the company.

## WHAT IS DISCRIMINATION?

Understanding that discrimination is illegal is especially important when it interferes with someone's ability to fairly get a job. The US Equal Employment Opportunity

Companies and employers are becoming more and more aware of how important it is to include disabled Americans to diversify and strengthen their workforce.

Commission (EEOC), which oversees hiring and employment practices in the country, specifically details which forms of discrimination in the workplace are against the law. The EEOC also lists hiring practices that are considered illegal because they can be considered forms of discrimination.

For example, employers may not ask for a photograph of a job applicant until after the decision has been made to offer the person a job and the applicant has accepted the offer. It is also against the law to consider many aspects of a job applicant's life when hiring:

# COINING THE TERM "ABLEISM"

How old is the term "ableism"? While many people are only now becoming familiar with it, it is hardly new.

In fact, the *Oxford English Dictionary* traces the word "ableism" back to 1981, when it was used in an issue of *Off Our Backs*, a feminist publication that was produced between 1970 and 2008: "'Ableism' that is, the systemic oppression of a group of people because of what they can or cannot do with their bodies or minds is the result of ... ignorance." It is not surprising that feminist scholars were the first to identify the system of ableism because they were also aware of and working to confront discrimination against women.

The term "ableism" is decades old, not a recent invention. Discrimination

**off our backs**

volume xi, number 5
May 1981
Washington, D.C.

**75¢ a women's news journal**

special issue:
women with disabilities

The word "ableism" was first used in this 1981 issue of *Off Our Backs*, a feminist magazine that promoted awareness of discrimination.

against the disabled has been referred to in the past by other terms, such as discrimination against the "differently abled" or "disability discrimination." Ableism is a fusion of the terms "abled" (those without disability) and the concept of the "-ism," inclusive of "racism" and "sexism" (terms for oppressive systems that favor people of a specific race or sex, respectively).

The term is now widely used to identify the ways in which people with disabilities face a number of obstacles to life, liberty, and the pursuit of happiness.

The solution here is to eliminate individual desks and instead provide tables with separate chairs; abled students can use the chairs while disabled users can simply sit at the tables in their wheelchairs. Here's another scenario: Are the bathroom sinks too high for someone in a wheelchair to reach the faucet? The solution is to make sure that at least one or more (or all!) sinks and counters are lowered to a height that is manageable for everyone.

The problem is that the school and the architects believe they have accommodated people with disabilities because they have built a ramp for them to enter the building; they have failed to consider ways in which wheelchair users must also be able to be present in the building, use its facilities, and teach and learn like everyone else.

# MYTHS AND FACTS

**MYTH**
Disability means inability.

Fact
When a person has a disability, that does not mean he or she cannot perform the task at hand. For example, an amputee with a prosthetic leg can play a basketball game, and a blind person can use a specialized keyboard to write his or her reports.

**MYTH**
Disability is a defect.

Fact
A disability is not proof that something is "wrong" with or defective about a person. Many people with disabilities feel that their particular disability is simply a facet of who they are and an important part of their identity. Viewing a disability as a defect means that you consider being abled as the "correct" way of being.

**MYTH**
Disabled people want your sympathy.

Fact
Disabled people have likely been the subject of condescending treatment for much of their lives. What they need is your respect and your willingness to treat them fairly. It is important that you not rush to help people you perceive to be in need; it is likely that they don't need it. If they do, they will ask you for it—don't assume, because then you are treating them as if they are helpless.

# CHAPTER TWO

# THE HISTORY OF ABLEISM

One of the most well-known proponents for disability rights in the modern era was Christopher Reeve, the American actor who played the iconic role of Superman in several hit movies. Reeve was an avid horseback rider, but in May of 1995, he was severely injured when he was thrown off his horse during a competition. His spine was damaged, paralyzing him from the neck down. He became a quadriplegic, which means that his paralysis affected all four limbs.

Despite the emotional devastation he experienced, Reeve soon became an outspoken advocate for the disabled. He made a decision to be very public about what people with disabilities such as himself endured. With his wife, he founded the Christopher and Dana Reeve Paralysis Resource Center, which teaches paralyzed people how to live independently. He also became chairperson of the American Paralysis Association and vice chairperson of the National Organization on Disability, and he helped advocate and raise funds for both organizations.

In 1996, he narrated a film, *Without Pity: A Film About Abilities*, which won an Emmy Award for Outstanding Informational Special. That year, *Time* magazine featured Reeve on its cover as a tribute to his activism on behalf of people with disabilities.

Hollywood star Christopher Reeve was paralyzed in a horseback-riding accident. He became one of the most outspoken advocates for disability rights in the United States.

Reeve died in 2004. For many Americans, his activism marked one of the first times they saw the rights of disabled people being highlighted. However, the disability rights movement is much older than 1995.

## RECOGNITION FOR DISABILITY RIGHTS

In the American colonies, people with disabilities were cared for—to varying degrees—by private organizations, such as churches. However, the federal government first took action to support people with disabilities in 1798. That year, President John Adams signed an act granting relief for sick and injured seamen—which means that disabled military veterans were some of the first Americans to have their rights recognized.

More progress was made in the 1800s. Benjamin Rush, the father of American psychiatry, published findings on mental disorders, recognizing them as a medical condition. In 1817, Thomas Gallaudet founded the Connecticut Asylum for the Education and Instruction of Deaf and Dumb Persons in Hartford, Connecticut. It was the first institution established to teach people

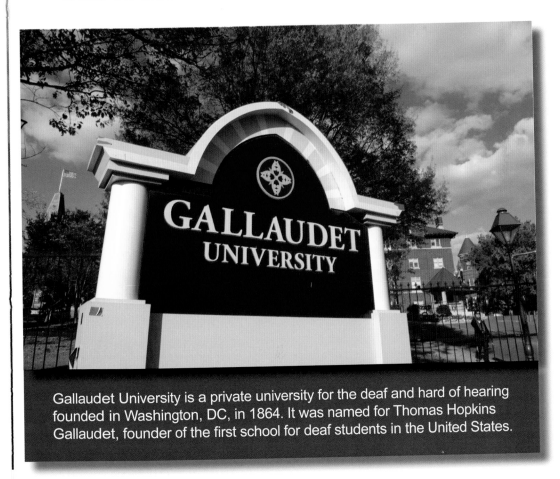

Gallaudet University is a private university for the deaf and hard of hearing founded in Washington, DC, in 1864. It was named for Thomas Hopkins Gallaudet, founder of the first school for deaf students in the United States.

# MICROAGGRESSIONS

Sometimes people discriminate against disabled people in smaller, but no less hurtful, forms called microaggressions. "Microaggressions" was a term first used to describe a particular form of racism. It was coined by Dr. Derald Wing Sue, who wrote, "Microaggressions are the brief and commonplace daily verbal, behavioral, and environmental indignities, whether intentional or unintentional, that communicate hostile, derogatory, or negative … slights and insults to the target person or group."

A common example involves racism: if a white person asks an Asian American "Where are you from?" he or she is assuming that the Asian American could not have been born in the United States; perhaps, even, it could be taken as a signal that "you don't belong here."

Disabled people face microaggressions every day. Consider these comments and questions that they hear:

- "You don't look like you have a disability." (Dismissing the disability.)
- "Everyone has some kind of problem." (Trivializing the disability.)
- "I am so OCD about my work!" or "My fear of heights is crippling!" (Joking about real disabilities.)
- Raising one's voice when speaking to a blind person (Assuming that if one sense is negatively affected, they all are.)

- "But you seem so intelligent." (Assuming disability can be equated to lack of intelligence.)
- "Why should you get a special accommodation? Either you can do the job or you can't." (Asserting that people are not entitled to legal accommodations and assuming that people should be defined and confined by their disabilities.)
- Encouraging a disabled person to do something he or she physically or emotionally cannot do, which is cruel. (For example, trying to get a person in a wheelchair to stand.)
- "Wow! You did it. You're so brave." (Making a big deal when a disabled person performs an everyday task.)
- "What would he like to drink?" (Addressing someone else rather than the disabled person him- or herself.)

Geri Jewell first became famous in *The Facts of Life* (1980–1984), becoming the first person with a visible disability to have a regular role in a prime-time series and the first actor with cerebral palsy to be featured on a TV series.

# HOW TO CONFRONT ABLEISM IN SOCIETY AND POPULAR CULTURE

It is not easy to stand up to ableism, especially in a social setting. Nobody wants to feel that he or she is complaining about unfair treatment, but the fact is that people need to be made aware that they are promoting ableism. So, what can you do?

First of all, speak up! There is nothing wrong with pointing out to an event planner that his or her plans have led to the exclusion of one or more people. It is important that abled and disabled people alike point these facts out. Consider the incident as a teachable moment. In this example, call the event planner and explain why it would be difficult for you or someone you know to attend the event. If he or she says something offensive, such as, "Wow, you don't look like you have a disability!" ask how many people with disabilities he or she knows. Inform the planner that he or she probably knows more disabled people than he or she imagines because many disabilities are invisible.

On the other hand, if a person offers to help and shows excessive concern where it is not needed, kindly tell him or her that if you need help, you will ask for it. This may help the person understand that disabled people are not incapable of helping themselves. Boundaries need to be respected, no matter what a person's status: abled or disabled.

There will be times when a more formal complaint is in order. If you have purchased tickets to a concert, for example, and find that the facility makes it difficult or impossible for you or your friends to access, you have the right to lodge a complaint. Remember that no matter

It is important to remember to treat disabled people with respect so that socializing will be a fun time for all. Be inclusive; you can choose to go somewhere else if a venue does not accommodate everyone in your group.

the disability, you are within your legal rights to enjoy a social or cultural event as much as anyone else.

Boycott programs, performances, or artists that you feel portray disability in a stereotypical way. Better yet, write letters and create petitions to make the producers and artists aware of how they are promoting ableism in popular culture. In addition, support and help promote programs and artists that you feel portray disability accurately and meaningfully.

If you are a creative person, produce art and literature yourself! Make your own YouTube channel that portrays disabilities accurately or write stories and poems in which disabled characters have agency.

# CHAPTER FOUR

# ABLEISM AT SCHOOL

People with disabilities had to fight hard for the right to equal education. For years, people like Helen Keller made it clear that children with disabilities, even multiple disabilities, had the right to learn and could lead fulfilling lives if afforded a good education. The fact is that some students still suffer from discrimination in their school settings.

## WHAT DOES ABLEISM LOOK LIKE IN THE CLASSROOM?

Many times, discrimination looks like sympathy but it is actually condescending behavior. A teacher may excuse a student from a test or an activity because he or she doesn't want to make the student feel bad if he or she cannot succeed at the task. The student, instead, feels worse because he or she has been left out of an activity and denied a chance to participate. The teacher may even be denying the student an opportunity to learn.

In another situation, a school may plan a field trip and decide that it cannot guarantee the safety and monitoring of a disabled student on the trip; as a result,

Actor Dan Aykroyd (*right*) has spoken about how living with Asperger syndrome has helped him with various roles, such as relating to the script during the making of *Ghostbusters* (1984). Here, Aykroyd is pictured alongside costar Bill Murray.

the school does not allow the student to attend and instead creates an alternate activity for him or her. This might constitute discrimination because the student should be able to attend the trip with an accommodation.

A school is planning a production or play. A disabled child would like to participate but is told he or she cannot because his or her behavior, which is the result of autism, is disruptive. This could constitute discrimination, as the school could, again, find an alternative way for the student to participate.

What if a student who has dyslexia is taking a timed examination? Time runs out before the student, who needs extra time to read and write, can finish the test, and he or she receives a failing grade as a result. This is discrimination because the failure is a result of inadequate time rather than a reflection of the student's ability.

Another example: a disabled student is told he or she cannot attend a particular school because the school cannot accommodate his or her special needs. This is obviously discrimination, as schools are obligated to meet the needs of disabled students.

Sometimes ableism is perpetrated not by the school and its administrators and teachers, but by other students. Disabled students may be suffering from harassment and bullying by other students or made to be the subject of hurtful jokes and comments about their disabilities. More often, they are left out of the school's social environment, discouraged from joining clubs because nobody wants to accommodate their disability, and left feeling isolated in a sea of their peers.

# BULLYING AND DISABLED STUDENTS

Studies show that students with disabilities are two to three times more likely than other students to suffer from bullying and harassment at school. The bullying can take place outside of the school as well, in clubs and after-school activities. Bullying, as we know, can affect a student's self-esteem and cause him or her to feel unsafe and insecure, which impacts well-being and academic success.

A graduate student at Michigan State University takes her guide horse with her to classes. This miniature horse named Cali trained to be a guide animal for blind people.

*(continued on the next page)*

*(continued from the previous page)*

According to the National Bullying Prevention Center, "Many students with disabilities are already addressing challenges in the academic environment. When they are bullied, it can directly impact their education."

What can schools and fellow students do? Intervening during a bullying incident is important, but so is generally showing more awareness and acceptance of students with disabilities. Disabled students are picked on more frequently because they are generally more isolated than abled students. A positive environment is one in which abled students and disabled students interact freely, where they sit together at lunch, hang out together at recess, and learn together in the same classrooms.

Disabled students should not be separated from the rest of the student body because this will cause them to be further isolated. As much as possible, they should be integrated within the routines, life, and culture of their schools.

## HOW TO CONFRONT ABLEISM AT SCHOOL

The Americans with Disabilities Act speaks very clearly about discrimination. The law protects anyone with "a physical or mental impairment which substantially limits one or more life activities." Activities like learning, reading, thinking, and communicating are "life activities," and as these are obviously conducted in a school setting, students are protected by the ADA.

Another law, the Individuals with Disabilities Education Act (IDEA), goes further; it ensures students with disabilities are provided with free appropriate public education (FAPE) that is tailored to their individual needs. IDEA covers students who have a disability and, as a result of that disability, need special education in order to make progress in school. In other words, some disabled students may not qualify for FAPE; if a student uses a wheelchair

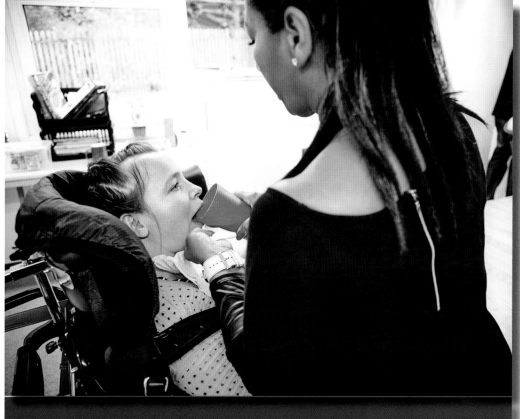

A caretaker helps a disabled girl drink water from a cup at the school where she is enrolled. Some students may require an aide or caregiver to accompany them in their learning environment.

but is succeeding academically at school, then he or she may not be covered under IDEA.

Some disabled children may need an aide with them to help them move through the building, help with their toileting needs, help them access certain facilities, serve as note takers, etc., and they are legally entitled to this service. In extreme cases, if a public school cannot provide a child an equal education because its resources or facilities are inadequate, then the school system must place that child in a school specially tailored to his or her needs.

If you notice discrimination in your own school, there are several things you should do. First, tell a trusted adult, such as your parents or guardians.

Most schools and school districts have an education coordinator, a 504 coordinator (who handles issues related to Section 504 of the Rehabilitation Act), or other individual appointed by the school to handle disabilities issues. This person should be updated on what is happening and be briefed on what the student's situation is, what the student's disability is, and what he or she will need to be successful. This coordinator may be able to resolve the issue, especially if it's an issue of the administration or staff not fulfilling their duties.

In an extreme situation, if a school will not comply with the student's legally entitled needs, it could help to contact the Office of Civil Rights for the Department of Education (OCR). The OCR offers resources to protect the needs of students and ensure that schools do not discriminate against disabled students. Its website provides information about how to file a complaint against a school.

What if you witness a disabled student being bullied or harassed by another student or group of students? Studies show that other students like yourself can actually be more effective than adults in putting a stop to bullying.

First of all, bullies usually know how to hide their behavior from teachers and other adults. It will be other students who witness bullying more frequently. Second, according to the National Bullying Prevention Center, bullying is 50 percent more likely to stop when a fellow student intervenes: "Peer advocacy—students speaking out on behalf of others—is a unique approach that empowers students to protect those targeted by bullying."

But remember: Do not put yourself in harm's way. If there is something physically violent happening, it is urgent that you alert a staff member right away. In these situations, you will be more helpful to the person being bullied if you get him or her the help needed.

# 10 GREAT QUESTIONS
## TO ASK A GUIDANCE COUNSELOR

1.  How does the school handle bullying?

2.  Will you keep our conversation confidential?

3.  What are my rights if I am being harassed or bullied?

4.  How can I protect myself or others from bullies?

5.  Can you be there with me if I confront the person who is bothering me (or another student)?

6.  What are my rights in terms of my education?

7.  My teachers are not cooperating. Can you help me resolve this?

8.  What can the school provide in terms of services to help each student succeed?

9.  Will it be on my record if I require accommodations?

10. What accommodations does my Individualized Education Program (IEP) allow me to have?

# CHAPTER FIVE

# ABLEISM AT WORK

I t is very important to recognize that ableism exists in the current American workplace. In fact, being unable to work and to be productive is a reason why so many disabled people are at a socioeconomic disadvantage. In other words, people who have one or more disabilities are at greater risk of being poor.

## WHAT ABLEISM LOOKS LIKE IN THE WORKPLACE

Discrimination in the workplace is sometimes difficult to detect. According to the organization Workplace Fairness, "Disability discrimination can occur in many ways. It can be direct, and obvious, or indirect, and not so obvious." For example, a person with a facial deformity is not served in the main eating area of a restaurant so that his appearance will not upset other diners. Or, in another example, a disabled veteran becomes a finalist for a job, but after seeing a photograph of him, the company opts to hire someone else. These examples are clearly discriminatory.

However, what about a situation in which a supervisor makes a PowerPoint presentation to employees that uses a small font in a pale color, which makes it very difficult to read? That would also be discriminatory because it prevents an employee who is visually impaired from benefiting from the information. However, this second example is more subtle and difficult to detect; someone may say it is merely thoughtless, rather than discriminatory. However, under the law, it would constitute discrimination if someone were to come forward about it.

A sign language interpreter translates a talk being given at a training seminar, making the event accessible for the hearing impaired.

Sometimes ableism becomes apparent before a person is even hired. The law states that an employer cannot ask about your physical health during a job interview. (An employer may ask you if you can perform certain duties of the job; for example, if you are applying for a job in a restaurant, the restaurant owner is allowed to ask if you are able to stand on your feet for eight hours a day without accommodation.) Neither can an employer ask you to take a physical examination to test your abilities before making a job offer.

Often, disabled people confront ableism while they are employed. In fact, ableism may become apparent soon after one begins working for a new employer. For example, a supervisor may decide to hold a staff meeting at a new location—a spontaneous outdoor meeting because the weather is sunny—but this new location cannot accommodate a person who uses a cane. The employee brings this to the attention of the supervisor, but the supervisor chooses the same location the following month. The supervisor is now discriminating against the disabled employee because these meetings are required, but they are held in a place that is not accessible. The employee wants to attend the meetings, but the supervisor's choice of location is making attendance impossible. This is not thoughtless behavior; it is illegal.

In another example, a disabled person may find herself working with someone who harasses her because of that disability. If a person suffers from anxiety and keeping his desk in a certain arrangement helps him feel calm, a coworker or employer might deliberately mess with the order of his workspace in order to upset him, thinking his reaction is funny. This is clearly harassment and should be acted upon because it can make the workplace a hostile environment.

# WHAT'S ESSENTIAL?

One aspect of identifying discrimination in the workplace is identifying what essential functions are. Every job has essential functions: for example, a server in a restaurant must be able to stand on his or her feet for long periods of time and carry heavy trays. These could be considered "essential functions" of the job of a server, and if a person is unable to perform these tasks, an employer may deny that person a job.

However, the employer must also determine if there is a reasonable accommodation that could be made to aid the server in performing the job: for example, can a rolling cart be provided so that heavy trays can be pushed

Employers must, under the law, attempt to make a reasonable accommodation for employees to help them perform required duties. A seated cashier dispenses tickets at a movie theater.

to diners' tables rather than carried by hand? If so, then this would be a reasonable accommodation and the server would be able to continue performing his or her job. Under the Americans with Disabilities Act, employers must provide reasonable accommodations that will help a disabled person perform the duties that are part of the job.

Some accommodations might be deemed unreasonable. For example, if a server in a restaurant has a speaking disability, it might be unreasonable to provide a translator to help that server communicate with diners or to communicate orders to kitchen staff. It might put too much of a burden on an employer, in which case the restaurant owner is not required to keep the server as an employee.

## WHAT YOU CAN DO ABOUT IT

If you are differently abled yourself, it is important for you to inform your employer that you feel you are being discriminated against by a certain policy, practice, or person. It is possible that your employer may deny the discrimination, but you must still articulate it. Your job is not to make your employer feel better about himself or herself, but to protect your own rights.

Start a paper trail so that you have documentation. Ask your employer to make a report about the discrimination so that there is a record, but also keep a diary in which you write down: 1) the date of the incident, 2) the names and titles of the people involved,

If you feel you have been discriminated against because of your disability, it is essential that you keep a record of all events and conversations related to the incident.

3) a summary of the incident in as much detail as possible, including the names of people who possibly witnessed it, and 4) a summary of the actions you have taken and reports you have made. Also, keep copies of any emails, letters, or other communications you have sent or received that relate to the incident.

What if you were not the subject of ableism but witnessed it happening to a coworker? Much of the same advice here applies: tell your employer what you witnessed, write down and document as much of the incident as you can, and contact the Equal

Employment Opportunity Commission (EEOC) if you need to do so. Let the person who is being impacted by discriminatory behavior know that he or she can depend on your support.

Find and look over your employer's antidiscrimination policy, whether it is on the company website, in an employee handbook, or in some other format. Make a copy of it and keep it because the fact that your employer has put that policy in writing will help you make your case.

Remember, an employer is obligated to maintain a workplace that is accessible for everyone and that prohibits discrimination against anyone with a disability. That means that you cannot be fired or penalized in any way for bringing discriminatory behavior to the attention of your employer.

If you feel that the situation is not being rectified, consider making a report to the EEOC, which oversees compliance for many federal antidiscrimination and antiharassment laws. There is a process through which you can file a charge—not a lawsuit—against your employer. This is an act that will get a government agency involved in your situation, and it will likely make your employer pay attention. There are also state agencies that can help you protect your rights in the workplace.

# CHAPTER SIX

# COPING WITH ABLEISM IN YOUR OWN LIFE

I t is easy to forget how much our culture and society present abled people as the norm, and disabled people as outsiders. But Linda Williams and Monica Slabaugh write about how rooted ableism is in our culture: "Ableism is a pervasive and historically preserved worldview that has led us to build discriminatory and oppressive infrastructures within the spaces we inhabit, the everyday language we use, and the programs we do and do not support as a culture."

## TAKE CARE OF YOUR INNER SELF

Ableism often causes disabled people themselves to internalize some of these stereotypes. As a disabled person, you may sometimes ask yourself questions like, "Come on, of course you can lift that box! Why don't you just try?" or "Why are you making a big deal about there being no bathroom for disabled people? If you can't attend, just say no."

Resisting those thoughts is necessary because they can make you feel that you don't deserve any accommodations or that you shouldn't make your

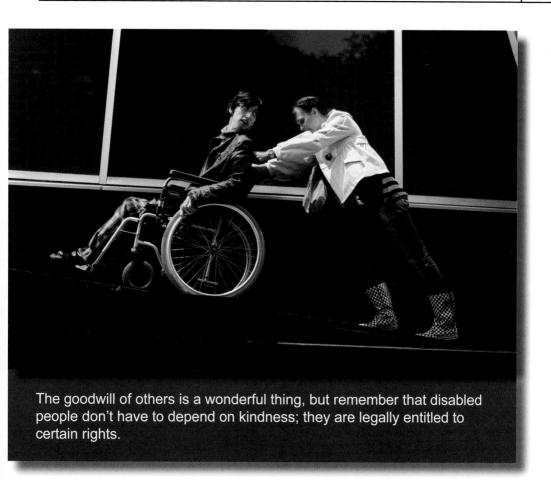

The goodwill of others is a wonderful thing, but remember that disabled people don't have to depend on kindness; they are legally entitled to certain rights.

situation into someone else's problem. However, remember that your comfort is not dependent on someone else's goodwill; it is your legal right, in many situations, to be accommodated.

Of course, it is easier to understand this logically than to manage it emotionally. If you find yourself plagued by uncomfortable internal thoughts, a good trick is to pretend that someone else is saying these things to you. When you imagine such words coming from someone else's mouth, you will realize that your nagging thoughts are really just extensions of ableist culture.

# INVISIBLE DISABILITIES

The ADA states that "a person is considered to have a disability if he or she has difficulty performing certain functions (seeing, hearing, talking, walking, climbing stairs, lifting, or carrying), or has difficulty performing activities of daily living, or has difficulty with certain social roles." However, some people live with disabilities that are not immediately apparent to others.

These conditions make it difficult or impossible for those people to perform their daily functions, even if the condition is not obvious to others. For example, some people suffer from pain that debilitates them, or they may regularly experience fatigue or dizziness. Sometimes, a person has suffered a brain injury or a back injury that makes moving through their daily routine almost impossible. Learning differences are

A young girl with dyslexia wears specially designed yellow glasses, which have filters that improve her visual perception—thus enabling her to read more easily.

another example of a disability, in which a child may need reasonable accommodations to learn (although an untrained person may not realize it when looking at the child).

Invisible disabilities are especially challenging to cope with because others often judge us based on what they can see. If they do not see a disability (a wheelchair, a cane, a brace, or some other assistive device), then they assume a person is able to perform all functions.

Speaking up for oneself is especially vital when your disability is invisible to others. Name the condition and state it clearly: "I have a back injury that prevents me from carrying that box," for example.

Surround yourself with people who support you and who want you to fulfill your goals. Make sure to avoid, as much as possible, people who make you feel that you are identified solely by your disability, no matter how well intentioned those people think they may be.

## TAKE ACTION TO CONFRONT ABLEISM

As stated earlier, discriminating against someone with a disability is not only thoughtless and insulting, it is also against the law. In almost every situation—school, work, civil society—there is a process in place for stopping it.

In school, be sure to report the discrimination to someone in authority: a teacher, administrator, guidance counselor, or another adult. You may also consult your statewide ADA compliance counselor.

At work, report the discrimination to your supervisor and, if needed, to human resources.

In a social setting, report the discrimination as soon as possible to someone in charge. For example, if you feel you or someone you know is being discriminated against in a restaurant or a theater, ask to see the manager right away.

What about those social situations in which it is not possible to report the offender to anyone? What if you are made to feel ostracized or isolated because of your

A teacher, administrator, or guidance counselor can all be excellent resources if you suspect discrimination. You should also consult your statewide ADA compliance counselor.

disability, or when your feelings have been deeply injured by someone's thoughtlessness?

One suggestion is that you confront the person by speaking up for yourself. If you are in a wheelchair and approach a cashier with a question, and that cashier responds to your abled friend instead of you, say something. Be polite, but firm: "Excuse me, but I am the one who asked you the question. Please address your response to me." If you are the abled friend in this situation, you can be equally mindful that your friend is being discriminated against. Ask the cashier to address the person who asked the question, and encourage your friend to continue to stand up for himself or herself. You may feel that you are embarrassing the cashier, but try not to worry about that: you and your friend are not being rude. You're simply pointing out someone's thoughtlessness and challenging his or her assumption. This is, in fact, a very brave thing to do.

# GLOSSARY

**ableism** A system or culture in which disabled people experience discrimination.

**accessibility** The quality of being easy to use, enter, or participate in.

**agency** The ability to act independently and use free will to make one's own choices.

**Americans with Disabilities Act (ADA)** A federal law that prohibits discrimination on the basis of disability in employment, public services, public accommodations and services operated by private entities, and telecommunications.

**antidiscrimination law** A law made regarding the right of people to be treated fairly and equally.

**condescending** An attitude that seems well intended on the surface but has the effect of being patronizing or implying one's superiority over another.

**confronting** Standing up and facing a situation in which you are being unjustly treated.

**disability** A mental, emotional, or physical condition that limits a person's movements or facilities.

**essential function** An aspect of one's job that is considered vital; for example, a speechwriter must be able to read and research documents.

**free appropriate public education (FAPE)** A term used to describe an educational program that is customized to meet the needs of students with learning differences to ensure they receive a satisfactory and standardized level of education.

**harassment** Aggressive behavior toward a person with the intent of intimidating or insulting him or her.

**impairment**  A complete or partial loss of an ability; hearing impairment is a loss of the ability to hear, while speech impairment is difficulty in communication and related areas.

**Individuals with Disabilities Education Act (IDEA)**  A federal act that ensures students with a disability are provided with education that is tailored to their individual needs.

**invisible disability**  A disability that is not readily apparent to someone who is untrained or unaware, such as a back injury or fibromyalgia.

**learning difference**  A difference in the way a person gains knowledge and learns information, such that accommodations usually need to be made for the person to succeed academically.

**lobotomy**  An outdated medical procedure in which part of the frontal lobe of the brain is removed, in an effort to cure mental disorders.

**paralysis**  A condition in which a person cannot move one or more limbs or other body parts.

**quadriplegic**  The affliction of being paralyzed in all four limbs (arms and legs).

**reasonable accommodation**  A provision made by an employer that will help a person with a disability complete his or her job duties, without resulting in significant detriment to the workplace.

# FOR MORE INFORMATION

The Arc of the United States
1825 K Street NW, Suite 1200
Washington, DC 20006
(202) 534-3700 / (800) 433-5255
Facebook: @thearcus
Twitter: @thearcus
Website: https://www.thearc.org
The Arc is an organization that advocates for and
    serves people with intellectual and developmental
    disabilities and their families.

Council of Canadians with Disabilities (CCD)
909-294 Portage Avenue
Winnipeg, MB R3C 0B9
Canada
(204) 947 0303
Email: ccd@ccdonline.ca
Facebook: @ccdonline
Twitter: @ccdonline
Website: http://www.ccdonline.ca
The CCD is a national human rights organization of
    people with disabilities working for an inclusive and
    accessible Canada.

The Institute on Disability Culture
11760 San Pablo Ave 302
El Cerrito, CA 94530
Website: http://www.instituteondisabilityculture.org
The institute's mission is to promote pride of the
    history, activities, and cultural identity of individuals

with disabilities throughout the world. Its website provides information about and shares examples of disability culture.

Learning Disabilities Association of Canada (LDAC)
2420 Bank Street, Suite 20
Ottawa, ON K1V 8S1
Canada
(613) 238-5721
Email: info@ldac-acta.ca
Facebook: @ldacacta
Twitter: @ldacacta
Website: http://www.ldac-acta.ca
The LDAC was founded in 1963 and is an advocate for people with learning disabilities and their caretakers. It works on preventing, identifying, and raising awareness of learning disabilities.

The National Consortium on Leadership and Disability for Youth (NCLD/Y)
c/o Institute for Educational Leadership
4301 Connecticut Avenue NW, Suite 100
Washington, DC 20008-2304
(877) 871-0744
Website: http://www.ncld-youth.info
The NCLD/Y is a national resource center led by young people to train and educate others about the rights of disabled Americans. Its goal is to produce a new generation of leaders to promote the disability rights movement.

US Equal Employment Opportunity Commission (EEOC)
131 M Street NE
Washington, DC 20507
(202) 663-4900
Facebook: @USEEOC
Twitter: @USEEOC
Website: https://www.eeoc.gov
> The EEOC is charged with ensuring that employers comply with federal employment regulations. It enforces the laws that prevent discrimination in the workplace.

## WEBSITES

Because of the changing nature of internet links, Rosen Publishing has developed an online list of websites related to the subject of this book. This site is updated regularly. Please use this link to access this list:

http://www.rosenlinks.com/SPKUP/Ableism

# FOR FURTHER READING

Best, Cynthia. *Meet ME Where I'm At!* Arlington, TX: Future Horizons, 2017.

Bodden, Valerie. *Helen Keller: Educator, Activist & Author* (Essential Lives). North Mankato, MN: Essential Library, 2016.

Burcaw, Shane. *Not So Different: What You Really Want to Ask About Being Disabled*. New York, NY: Roaring Brook Press, 2017.

Draper, Sharon. *Out of My Mind*. New York, NY: Atheneum Books for Young Readers, 2010.

Libal, Autumn. *Deaf and Hard of Hearing* (Living with a Special Need). Broomall, PA: Mason Crest, 2014.

Morganelli, Adrianna. *Rick Hansen: Improving Life for People with Disabilities* (Remarkable Lives Revealed). New York, NY: Crabtree, 2016.

Moss, Wendy, and Susan Taddonio. *The Survival Guide for Kids with Physical Disabilities and Challenges*. Golden Valley, MN: Free Spirit Publishing, 2015.

Palacio, R. J. *Wonder*. New York, NY: Knopf, 2012.

Philip, Aaron. *This Kid Can Fly: It's About Ability (NOT Disability)*. New York, NY: Balzer + Bray, 2016.

Twiss, Johan. *Trapped in My Mind Palace.* New York, NY: Twiss Publishing, 2016.

# BIBLIOGRAPHY

Americans with Disabilities Act of 1990, As Amended. Full text. Retrieved April 17, 2017. https://www.ada.gov/pubs/adastatute08.htm.

Anna. "What Is Ableism? Five Things About Ableism You Should Know." November 19, 2010. http://disabledfeminists.com/2010/11/19/what-is-ableism-five-things-about-ableism-you-should-know.

Brinkerhoff, Shirley. *Why Can't I Learn Like Everyone Else?* (Youth with Disabilities). Broomall, PA: Mason Crest, 2004.

Charlton, James I. *Nothing About Us Without Us: Disability Oppression and Empowerment*. Berkeley, CA: University of California Press, 2000.

Danforth, Scot. *Becoming a Great Inclusive Educator* (Disability Studies in Education). New York, NY: Peter Lang, 2014.

Davis, Leonard. *The Disability Studies Reader*. Abingdon, UK: Routledge, 2006.

Hehir, Thomas, and Lauren I. Katzman. *Effective Inclusive Schools: Designing Successful Schoolwide Programs*. San Francisco, CA: Jossey-Bass, 2012.

History.com. "Civil Rights Act." Retrieved April 17, 2017. http://www.history.com/topics/black-history/civil-rights-act.

PACER. "Bullying and Harassment of Students with Disabilities." National Bullying Prevention Center. Retrieved April 17, 2017. http://www.pacer.org/bullying/resources/students-with-disabilities.

Smith, Laura, Pamela F. Foley, and Michael P. Chaney. "Addressing Classism, Ableism, and Heterosexism in Counselor Education." *Journal of Counseling*

*& Development*, Summer 2008, Volume 86, pp. 303–309.

US Department of Commerce. "Nearly 1 in 5 People Have a Disability in the US, Census Bureau Reports." US Census Bureau, July 25, 2012. http://www.census.gov/newsroom/releases/archives/miscellaneous/cb12-134.html.

US Equal Employment Opportunity Commission. "Prohibited Employment Policies/Practices." Retrieved April 17, 2017. https://www.eeoc.gov/laws/practices/index.cfm.

Williams, Linda, and Monica Slabaugh. "Invisible Disability Project: Ableism and Erasure." San Diego Free Press, March 23, 2016. http://sandiegofreepress.org/ 2016/03/invisible-disability-project-ableism-and-erasure.

Wolbring, Gregor. "The Politics of Ableism." *Development*, 2008, Volume 51, pp. 252–258.

Workplace Fairness. "Your Rights: Disability Discrimination." Retrieved April 17, 2017. http://www.workplacefairness.org/disability-discrimination.

# INDEX

## ABOUT THE AUTHOR

Susan Nichols has written a number of books about history, world cultures, and the arts and culture for young readers. She is especially interested in social justice issues and the ways in which people can improve the future by learning about history. She lives in Baltimore, Maryland, and is an English teacher.

## PHOTO CREDITS